Outline to Ending

How to Write Your First Book in 30 Days

Amy Pendergrass

CONTENTS

Introduction

Let's say you want to write a non-fiction book in a month. For argument's sake, let's also say that you only have a few hours to work on it every day and you've never written a book before.

At this point, you're probably wondering to yourself if that's even possible or if you are just setting yourself up for failure.

Well, let me relieve your mind by saying...YES it is *definitely* possible, even if you've never written a book before!

What's more is that in 30 days, you can write a *damn good book* that can generate a healthy passive income stream for you.

Professional writers (now we are speaking mostly of non-fiction writers) know that the secret to writing a well thought-out structured book quickly is to stay on point so your readers won't get angry or bored with your writing.

By following *Outline to Ending*, you will learn the exact methods professional writers use and how you can duplicate these techniques again and again and again.

Outline to Ending breaks the writing process down into steps, with timing and limits to place on yourself to keep you laser-focused on your goal.

Every one of us has at least one subject we feel we could write a fascinating book about. Maybe it's about how to build a redwood deck, or the Paleo diet, or the proper way to kick a football.

It used to be you'd have to write and research your topics, which could take years and dozens of visits to libraries, then worry about proper formatting of manuscripts, and then you had to get someone to actually publish the book!

But three technological advances have changed all that. The first was the personal computer, allowing anyone to quickly and easily format, well, anything. The second was the Internet, allowing for thousands of libraries worth of information to be called up at any moment. The third was the introduction of self-publishing and the advent of sites like Smashwords, Kindle Direct Publishing, and the iBook store. These three advances have made it possible for any organized person to publish a fantastic book in as little as 30 days.

Unfortunately, many people never start because they don't know how to organize their thoughts, research, and time. This book will help you overcome those obstacles by organizing your writing and research time into simple chunks spread out over 30 days even if you work a full-time job.

If you follow these steps and timelines, you'll be simply amazed on Day 30 as you stare at *your own* completed book!

Week 1 – The Research Phase

Week 1 is where it all begins. You'll be working toward a first draft, but before you can start down that path, you must pick a topic, do your research, and make your outline. These first seven days are the starting point, not only for determining your topic, but also for helping you set your time for the next four weeks!

Every day, you'll be spending a set amount of time for your research and writing. Try to stick to those suggested times. Not only will it make it easier to fit the plan into your life, but it will also give you an idea of your production rate. If you know you can only write 500 words in 90 minutes, you may find you need to work a little faster some days. One of the big things that keep people from completing their book is the fact that they leave things too far open. By putting limits on things, you'll be forced to direct your energies better.

Day 1 – Topic Development – 90 minutes

You know things. You have dozens of areas where you are an expert, which you can tell the world about and lead to a greater expanse of knowledge for the world. The only thing is, you need to figure out EXACTLY what it is you are going to write about. That can be one of the most difficult parts of the process, because if you don't get it right, you can find yourself waffling along and not actually getting any closer to producing that *best-selling book*!

Start your first day with a simple mind map. Think about what you do at work, the things you do around the house. You might find it easy to come up with five or six broad concepts, like 'Cooking' or 'Data Processing'. Write these down with a column underneath it, and then create a list of secondary things those broader tasks entail. Cooking may lead you to 'menu planning,' while Data Processing might lead you to 'spreadsheets'. Don't be afraid to make your list long, maybe 15 to 20 items, but remember that that will make it harder to zero-in on that one, perfect topic.

What you'll almost certainly discover is that the list of secondary topics for one or two of your broad categories will be much longer than the others. It's likely that those areas are the ones you've had the most exposure or the best understanding of. These tend to be the areas where you're most likely to strike gold in creating your book!

Next, take the area where you have the most secondary topics and start mapping out third-level topics underneath each secondary topic. After a while, look at those lists and you'll likely discover again that one or two are far more populated than the others. That secondary topic is likely the one that's perfect for your book! While an area like 'Cooking' might be appealing, it's so broad that you could never cover it in a single book, but menu planning is still wide enough to allow for interesting points to be made in a variety of areas, while still being contained enough to actually be coverable. That's the sweet spot, and it allows for further exploration of the topic in the future.

After you've brought it down to a manageable number, start to look into resources in the various areas you're thinking about writing in. Some will already have hundreds of books written about them, menu planning for instance, and some topics might be so granular that there may only be one or two books on them out there at all, and maybe even Google can't help you! With very few exceptions, you'll need to be able to research your topic and add secondary information from books, articles, and other sources. These are often the most important part of a book, and often it's by examining what others have said, and how they can contradict one another, that gives an author a new view on the proper direction for his book. Find a few sources for the topics you've come down to on your mind mapping.

That's 90 minutes. Try to stick close to it. One of the reasons for the time limit is that you can go deeply into research and end up spending hours and hours on that simple task.

Day 2 – Finalizing Your Topic – 90 minutes

Yesterday, you did all that work to suss out what you're going to write about. I'm proud that you've come this far. Settling on a topic is crucial. As much as you'd like to write multiple books at once, trying to do so will lead to confusion and typically kill both books before they're written. Today you'll narrow it to one topic.

Yesterday, you winnowed and you looked into the available research materials. It's probably obvious which one you should go for, but if there are still a couple to choose from, here's a good tie-breaker—go back to your original mind map and look at all your potential areas for writing. Now, look at how many are related to the topics you're trying to choose between. Almost certainly one of those has more. That's the one that has the deeper connection to your life. It may not look like it's a key part of your life, but it's so deeply connected.

And if you're still tied, just flip a coin.

OK, you now have a topic to write about. This single topic is now entirely what you're going to focus on during your writing time. Today, you're going to start reading up on your subject, and it should be pretty simple. Start by at least power-skimming those resources you discovered on your first pass through. That will help get you in the right direction. During this reading session, you don't have to absorb every word. You're not looking for details, you just want to understand the basics of the pieces you find. Are those pieces taking a different angle than you will? Do they mention other pieces that you can reference? Do they use examples that you are aware of? These are the basics that you should be looking at on this day.

You will be tempted to start writing, but this is not the time. I know, I know, you want to get in there and get your hands dirty, but you really need to get a slightly stronger base before you can go for it. Stick to your research phase and you'll be ready to hit the ground running!

Day 3 – Diving Deep – 90 minutes

Today, you start hardcore researching. I will say that this is the part where you'll discover the full extent of your knowledge on your topic. You'll start by doing every Web search you can think of surrounding your topic. You'll find thousands of hits, and some of them will no doubt already be familiar to you. That's a good thing! At this point, start taking notes. Lots of notes. Write down titles and use your browser's bookmarking options. You're going to want to refer to many of these sites again and again.

One of the keys to all of this is knowing what to trust. Anyone can say anything on the Internet, but you'll quickly discover ways to determine authentic research from someone spouting garbage. One way: whom do they cite? Reputable research institutions are good signs for a citation. Blog posts are less so. No citations are usually not worth looking at. Dig up many pieces with at least good provenance and get reading.

And reading.

And reading.

While you read, take notes. Give each article its own page, front and back, and start simply writing down the title, the online location, and the date. Those things will allow you to track back, and at some point, you'll need to track back to where all this information came from. After that, write down things that directly relate to your point of view on the topic, and anything that negates that point. Highlight those negations, as they are often points where a different point of view can actually make those things clearer and more applicable. After you've completely read the article, write a brief, one- or two-sentence summary, and specifically how YOU would have pitched the article. That will become quite important as the steps toward your book unfold!

Some tips for note taking:

- Don't write down numbers unless they are very important. Nothing will slow down the note-taking process more than copying down tables of numbers that, in the end, may not even have a bearing on your book. A note like "See table 1.1 at..." will allow you to access that information later if needed.
- Find clear messages. Make sure to write down not just specifics and details but the broader messages as well. That's the key to getting the most out of an article.
- Note the articles' citations. You'll likely want to go through and look at those references.
- Make note of the style. One thing you'll certainly want to know is if the works you're finding are done in an academic or a more casual or commercial style. This is important for a number of reasons, but largely because it will affect your writing style.

- Write or type clearly. Nothing is more frustrating than having notes you can't actually read!

Day 4 – Allow Me to Introduce Myself – 90 minutes

You know how I said you weren't going to be writing yet? Well, that ends today! You're not going to be tackling the meat of your topic. Instead, you're going to be clarifying your topic to yourself, and potentially to others. You're going to write your introduction.

A good introduction is not very long. Five hundred to a thousand words is ideal. You want to set out what the book will cover, give an idea of the tone of the book, and actually help you realize EXACTLY what you're writing about.

For this stage, all you want to do is start writing as if you're telling a friend about your book—what you'll be covering, what parts there'll be, how the entire thing will work. Unless you are specifically going for an academic or tutorial style, being conversational will help readers connect with you. Spend 50-60 minutes setting yourself up. Go over your notes, or maybe give something you read yesterday another look, or maybe there's something that you think would make a nice quote to open or end your introduction. I always start by asking myself "what the heck am I doing this for?" and then answering that in my introduction.

Write for at most 70 minutes. No more. You may find that you're not actually finished in that amount of time, and that's ok. You'll have many more chances at it. What's important is to get the words on the paper. Don't worry about grammar and spelling at this point, this is just getting the first words on paper. The key is to write in a way that clarifies your positioning.

Then...stop. No, don't go back and change that first paragraph around. No, don't do spell-check. No, you don't need to double-check the difference between microeconomics and macroeconomics. You're done. This was your first bit of writing and you did exactly what you needed to do. So now, relax!

Day 5 – Read, Read, Read!!! – 60+ minutes

This is the first of the work days where you may find yourself going deeper and deeper. Here, you're going to look for other books published in the area you're publishing. Go to the iTunes Bookstore, Kindle store, Smashwords, anywhere they feature books, and look for things related to your topic. Download them and start reading!

One of the reasons for this day is to recharge your batteries. If you're too focused on the creation side, you can easily poop-out and your book may never get written. If you're writing about your topic, you should also be seriously interested in it, and really, if you're not interested enough in your subject to get at least a little caught up in reading about it, maybe you've chosen the wrong topic!

Read for 60 minutes at least, maybe take some notes, but don't stress over it. This is a day of semi-rest, so you may take it a bit easy.

Day 6 – Even more Reading, Reading, Reading!!! – 60+ minutes

Again, this is sort of a relaxation day, where you dig into things more, and go into areas that might not be 100% your topic. Here, you're going to go slightly more afield, and for good reason. You're going hunting for trends.

Now before you say anything like '*But I don't want to be TRENDY!*,' you need to understand how people choose what books they're going to read. They start by doing searches, or by finding a store and browsing categories they are interested in. Finding items that are directly related to your topic is easy but often, people will come at your work from an angle that you weren't expecting! If you're planning to write that book on menu planning, for example, look up cookbooks or party-hosting guides or books on wine pairing. Here, you're not so much looking for content you can use in your book, but for an idea of what your books will be setting alongside.

This is also a great time to start finding trends. No matter what section of what store your book will be in, there are going to be trends, and it can actually be entirely helpful to find them and keep them in your mind. A lot of books with bright green covers might not mean that you use a green cover for your menu planning book, but maybe, just maybe, a vivid spring of parsley shows up. Or if there are a lot of books with long, in-depth chapters, you should remember that.

Most services offer information such as sales ranking, total reads, and popularity scores or user ratings. Find popular books and analyze them. Read comments. You don't have to write the exact same book, but often it's a good thought to keep your book in line with what else is out there.

Some trends to looks for:

- How long is the book? Are the books 5,000 words? 20,000?
- Are the books written with a lot of detail? Are there step-by-step sections or do writers tend to speak more generally?
- Are the books written in a casual tone or a formal one?
- What sort of external links and connections do they offer?
- Are there bullet point lists that give you tips on what to look for?

Just noting these things can help you connect with your readers and produce a better reading experience.

Day 7 – Your Outline – 120 minutes

Yesterday was about recharging for today. Today, you have two hours to put together your entire outline.

WHAT?!?!?! I hear you scream.

Yes, in two hours you will have an outline. A clear, simple, ready-to-use outline. You have to write an outline to produce your book, and here's a HUGE tip: no matter what, your book will have five chapters.

How do you know? I hear you ask.

It's simple: to properly tell a story, to properly instruct someone in something, to properly give enough of anything, you have to have a beginning, a middle, and an end. With five chapters, plus an introduction, you have a set-up piece, and the opener to give the most important information, the absolute basics. That allows for depth, and it's easy for readers to absorb what you're presenting in the five-chapter format. Remember: Shakespeare wrote everything in five acts.

Some authors prefer denser, more thorough outlines, which are an absolute must if you're writing fiction, but for non-fiction, you're likely better off going with a simpler, less detailed one. For example, my outline for this chapter looked something like this:

Week 1 – The Research Phase

Day 1 – 90 minutes
Topic Identification, Resource Discovery
  - Going through your knowledge base for concepts

- Looking for your best resources

Day 2 – 90 minutes
Reading Day, Topic Finalization
  - Pick what you're going to write about

Day 3 – 90 minutes
Detailed Research, Note-taking
  - Delve into your topic fully
  - Advice for taking notes

Day 4 – 120 minutes
Detailed Research, Note-taking, Introduction Writing
  - More note-taking advice
  - Writing intro to help focus research and planning

Day 5 – 60+ minutes
Reading, Reading, Reading!
  - Discovering other books in your topic
  - Reading semi-related works

Day 6 – 60+ minutes
Reading, Reading, Reading
  - Discovering even more books
  - How to read trends in publishing

Day 7 – 120 minutes
Outline writing
  - Tips for creating successful outlines (five chapters, pacing of chapters, avoiding unnecessary info dumps)

It's not expansive, and if you've read this far, you know that it's not 100% what you're reading now, is it? That's why it's an outline.

Start by writing titles for each portion of your book, even if there are more than five, and then go and provide some fill in those sections, which will give you an idea of what you're thinking about for that chapter.

Work on this for two hours. If you can't come up with an outline after six days of research and an intro at least mostly written, you probably shouldn't be writing a book.

After that, your first week is done. Congrats! You have an intro and an outline, you've studied your topic, you're ready to write and write and write, and starting on Day 8, you're going to be writing!

Week 2 – The First Draft

Week 2 is where the researcher becomes the writer. You're going to write your first draft, and that can be the most difficult part of the entire process. You go from almost nothing to very much something. You're not going to have a finished book at the end of the week, but you will have put the walls up!

Every day, you'll be spending a set amount of time writing. You're not going to be researching, except perhaps to double-check some specific quote or statistic, you're going to be putting your words into a word processor. You won't be editing; you'll just be writing. That's the key to making the 30 days work—spending a full week just writing.

Day 8 – Rewriting Your Introduction – 90 minutes

Remember all those days ago when you wrote your introduction? Well, you're going to do it again. What you want to do now is rewrite it using all the aspects you have picked up in your Days 5 and 6 reading. Unless you got lucky, you're going to want to address the things you noticed about those books you discovered this time. I wouldn't start by tossing out your first version; instead, read it and see what works and what doesn't. It's an essential skill to conquer—rewriting. It's about understanding that a wall needs to be torn down while still maintaining the integrity of the house. This day, you're rewriting the very first thing people will see when they open up your book.

Some tips:

- Don't start over! Instead, work within your document, making changes to it. If a 'Track Changes" function is available in the word processor you're using, make sure to use it.
- If you can, print a copy of the original and read it a couple of times. Work on a pass at the intro, read the original, then work some more, and read again. Seeing where you were can often lead you to where you need to get.
- Don't obsess over spelling and grammar, but do obsess over your voice. Come up with a tone and try to be consistent. That will help bring readers in and keep them reading.
- Don't stress! You got this.

Once you've rewritten the introduction, set it aside and don't look at it again. Don't fuss over it, don't do anything but save the file, close the application and spend your time doing something else.

Tomorrow's another day!

Day 9 – Writing Chapter 1 – 90 minutes

These days when you're writing a chapter are the most difficult. Not because writing is particularly hard, but because there's a part of your brain that is trying to stop you. It will do everything it can to stop you. It will make you sleepy. It will make television sound like the most entertaining thing in history. It will make you question what you're trying to do. It will distract you in every way possible, making every other activity seem more vital, more important, more fun.

That's why we have time allotments. No matter what that dastardly part of your brain keeps telling you, devote at least that limited amount of time to the writing and you'll certainly make it further than your brain will try to convince you that you can.

In Chapter 1, you're going to go further than you did in the intro. You're going to get into the meat of your book. Think about when you read a book. You read the introduction and it tells you what you're going to get and makes you want to get there. The first chapter actually moves you down the path. If you're writing a how-to book, this is where you go into the basics of what you'll need to get, and maybe a little bit of step-by-step in the basic techniques. If you're writing an exploration of a topic, let's say menu planning, you will start by looking at exactly what menu planning is and a bit on how it's done. If you're doing a tightly-focused topic, you can jump in a bit with the first chapter. If you're a little broader, you will use your first chapter to give the detailed look at the topic and how it works. This is where your outline will help. You'll see the direction and will almost certainly feel the amount you'll have to cover. That can be the hardest part—figuring out how much ground needs tilling. You'll figure it out by a couple of later steps.

Again, just write. Don't edit. Don't fuss over word choice or grammar, just try to write like you talk. It will help give readers a way to latch on to you by providing a personalized touch.

You'll find that first chapter done quickly if you're properly prepared!

Day 10 – Writing Chapters 2 and 3 – 120 minutes

This is the day. Today, you're writing two full chapters. This is the big day, though it does involve a question I get asked a lot: *how long does my book need to be?* I've heard hundreds of answers to that question. Long enough to cover the topic is a classic. I'm not that unkind. I'm going to tell you an actual answer:

5,000 to 10,000 words, leaning toward 5,000.

That's a far more specific number than most advisors will give you, but there's solid evidence behind it. First, there's the form. Yes, people read novels on their readers all the time, but it's still not the ideal reading situation. For your book, 5000 words are certainly doable for the first time writer, and if you discover you need more words, you can do that! Try to keep it shorter reading, unless you find that all the other books are in a much different length, then you might want to reconsider. Five thousand to ten thousand is easily doable in 30 days, though. Stick to that.

The real goal of this first writing week is to get the words out, and once they are out, you can deal with them accordingly a little later. You must first defeat the blank screen! The hardest part is making that first mark, committing words to screen. If you can do that, you'll end up winning.

The second chapter is an interesting point in your book. You've gone beyond all the preliminaries and have to deal with the absolute meat of the matter. Making it strong is essential, because the foundation only works if the house you build on it can stand. Here, you're going to want to give a sense of the book as a whole, and if you were to read it without the rest of the book, you'd still get an idea of what was going on. That's what you're dealing with in Chapter 2.

Chapter 3 is more of the same, but at this point you

should be trying to move the reader toward the end by showing them that they've already absorbed so much information. There are a lot of ways to do that—review moments, call-backs to early sections, or even just a phrase like "You might remember from Chapter Two..." will help keep the reader on track, and there's a sort of psychological payoff from reading something like that and actually remembering it!

Today you're writing two chapters. That seems like a lot, and honestly, it is. You're powering through this pass so you're going to have to stretch at times. Today, you want to write somewhere between 1,500 and 2,000 words. Not as many as you think. Look at it like writing a dozen medium-length emails to a friend. In fact, many folks have turned emails from friends into successful books (but I would recommend against it—not as easy as it sounds). Just start writing as if you're telling your book to someone, and keep going! You'll find a natural break point to settle each chapter, so just keep writing; you'll have lots of chances to go back and make fixes, but without the raw materials, you're sunk.

Day 11 – The Hard Chapter – 90 minutes

There is no harder chapter than the fourth chapter. It's not nearly the end, though the action has peaked, and it's not a part of the beginning. In baseball, it would be the set-up man, in for an inning to get things ready for the closer. Here, the work is toward conclusion, while not forgetting that there's always more to say.

Which brings up a very good point: never ramble. Yes, you can go on digressions, even taking the reader down the occasional rabbit hole, but if you're going to do that, you need to make sure you can tie it all back together to the main thread. Just including an anecdote that only lightly touches on your main topic is a likely way to lose your reader, though if it's fully tied in, with a good point that helps illuminate the main message, that can turn a casual reader into a major fan! On your first pass, maybe add one of these, and then maybe you'll find that it doesn't fit. That's why it's a first pass.

Two things to work on for Chapter 4. First is you must end the chapter as close to the finish as possible without actually being the finish. It's a game of inches. You must get close to the end or you may as well have it be Chapter 3, but if you go an inch over, it's Humpty-Dumpty all over again. Second, if you're not directing the reader back to segments of your book, you really should be. That is how you reinforce the key elements from earlier chapters and give the reader a solid set of direction as to the main messages.

Now, with all your writing, you should make sure you're being consistent. If you call it a kniflin pin in Chapter 1, don't go calling it a pin of kniflin in Chapter 4. Maintain these sorts of things and your reader will take away important messages.

Now, I'm saying to write for 90 minutes today, which is important for a number of reasons. Writing at a decent clip, 1,000 words an hour is not exactly difficult. Remember, just write and write and write. You will be going back and revising everything, so you don't have to be perfect. You do have to be fast, because nothing will help you finish your book like writing a first draft. Proving to yourself that you can do that will help ensure that you actually manage to do it!

At this point, you may also need a break. If you've written the chapter and you find yourself with time left over, go back over your notes. There's often something you're missing, and it's often at that point where you're nearing the end. The finish is pretty solid in most cases, as the beginning is right there staring at you, but sometimes it's in the lead-up to the finish that things can falter a bit. Take a moment and double-check.

Day 12 – The Final Chapter! – 120 minutes

Believe it or not, this is the day you finish your first draft. This day is special because you're breaking into three parts—writing, reading, and writing. It's simple, really, and you're going to nail it, but first, you need to think about two very important things.

First, what do you want your readers to walk away thinking? That's what your last chapter does. No matter what the topic, whether it's fiction or non-fiction, prose or poetry, your final chapter is what folks will remember. Work on it and it will make you memorable!

Second, look at what you hath wrought, and use that! Make sure that you actually remembered to hit every point you had on your outline. That can only be accomplished one way: by reading. You're going to write for 45 minutes today. That's not all, but it's the start. You may not be able to finish the final chapter, but there's a good chance you will. Write for 45 minutes, then go back and read everything you've written. It might take you 45 minutes, but it's certainly doable. After that, look at how everything hangs together...or doesn't. This will be the start of phase two!

Some things to remember for your final chapter:

- Don't merely recap all the other portions of the book. Add significant new material, even if only a little. Think of a recipe: the last line is usually something like "serves 7 to 10," which doesn't say much, but it does add to the overall product. Every book's final chapter should at least have that.
- Write a conclusion that not only sums up the chapter but the entire book. That will help leave your reader with a stronger impression and will allow you to

possibly even set up a sequel!

- But, most importantly, just finish the writing. Once you manage that, everything else becomes so much easier.

Day 13 – The Pass Back Through – 60 minutes

Well, you've written a first pass. Congrats! It's not done yet, not nearly done yet, but you've made a very good start toward having your very own book! The next step is to start molding it into a finer package, so you have to start reading and rereading. One of the reasons for a shorter book is that it can be read quickly, and that means you can read it twice in an hour!

This time, you're going to want your computer with the word processor application you're using (and honestly, I shouldn't have to tell you how much easier that makes things!) and a notebook or just some paper. Start by reading and noting every paragraph and the idea it's putting forth. For example, if I were making notes on this Day's writing, I'd read that first paragraph and write in my notes 'Important part - rewriting'. That's the level you want to go and do. Part of it is so that you can go back and compare the notes you take now with your outline. They should be very nearly the same! If they are, then you've managed it, but sometimes, you've strayed a few places. Once in a while, this is a good thing, but sometimes it does muddy the waters.

After you've read it once, do that comparison with your outline. Are there things missing? Did you add things? Are you happy with the order in which you put things? Do you want to move things around? All of that is what this pass is about.

In your second read through, look for clarity in the writing. There are going to be problems, no matter how thorough you were during the writing process, so just read for clarity on your second pass. Make sure each paragraph gets that message across unambiguously. That can be tricky, but tomorrow, you'll have a chance at making it work a lot easier.

Once you've read the book twice, set it down and go do something else. Tomorrow is a big day because it goes from being something you do to something that has been seen!

Day 14 – Find Foolish Friends – 60 minutes

This is the day you reveal to all the world what you have been working on. Well, not exactly. It's the day you find foolish friends to help you with the text and clarity passes you'll be doing. First, make a list of all your friends. Then really think about what they do. Do you have a friend who is an award-winning editor? That would be ideal! Most of us don't have that option, so you can go looking at folks who might write a lot, or who work in education, or who just seem very good at the whole English thing. They would make good potential readers for your manuscript. Choosing a friend who is always busy is probably not a great idea, as you're going to want to get started on this really soon. You'll probably hit on the right person early on, and often if you say to people, 'Hey, I'm writing a book, wanna help?' they're more than happy to help out, as long as you mention them in your acknowledgments!

You're going to want to get in touch with those friends today, and you're going to want to ask them if they can read your book for you in three or four days and send you feedback. What sort of feedback? Well, that depends on what your strengths are. If you're a master of grammar and syntax and spelling, you may want them to read for flow and context. If you're a dramatic writer, you may want them to deal with the technicalities of spelling and the like. Maybe you're just trying to make sure that folks understand what's going on, which is important. Decide what you want them to be reading for and ask them if they'll read it and get it back to you in a couple of days with notes. Tell them what you'd like them to focus on, but that they can make comments on everything. When they say yes, send them the manuscript and any specific things you'd like them to be on the lookout for. Maybe you want them to concentrate on the middle of the book or on a specific chapter. Mention that and they're sure to be on the lookout.

Once you've done that, it's time for your work on the mechanical part. Yes, you may not be the best person for checking the spelling and grammar, but at least some of it has to be you. Almost every word processor has a built-in spell-check, and mostly such a feature is pretty good, but sometimes you mean to type 'checker' but type 'checked' instead and that isn't going to be what the system understands! This is a careful reading, and you should not be afraid to look things up online. There are tons of great grammar resources online. Don't feel like you have to follow Strunk & White or AP style, but do remain consistent. Readers are often turned off from a book due to spelling mistakes, and those are easier to deal with. Just read carefully, and when you're in doubt, double-check. Spending a little extra time on the spell-check will help you come up with a better end product.

There is a mistake some writers make, and it's one of the reasons for the shorter day today. Do not needle your piece to death. Do your passes, but don't do 20 or 30. Take a couple and move on. Never overwhelm a full day with revising, instead spread it between several days doing shorter passes. That will give you a better view of what you've done and instead of fussing over every letter for hours on end, it'll allow you to come at the work with different eyes every day.

Besides, Week 3 is about taking your first draft and reworking it into a newer, better shape, ready to go!

Week 3 – The Re-Writening!

You've done your first draft, and now it's time to mold and remold the entire package. Why didn't you fuss over language and grammar when you were writing it the first time, thus saving you a step? Because it would have saved you a step. Getting fresh eyes on the piece every time is utterly important, and by having to rework with the piece more than once, you come at it with different ideas and tactics.

At the end of the week, you'll be ready for the finishing touches, but first comes a period a lot of writers foolishly neglect. This is where you look at the 'shape' of your book. You will discover that, as is, the book will have bulged in some areas, remained too narrow in others. That's what this week is about.

Day 15 – Reshaping – 90 minutes

Today, you're going meta! You're going to be looking at how successfully you have dealt with your topic overall. You're going to start by reading your outline again. Then you're going to read your book, start to finish. No notes, no cross-referencing, just read it. Now, after you've done that, you're going to do something a bit strange.

You're going to review your book.

After you've read your book, write the outline of the book again, but this time from the point-of-view of someone reading the book and reviewing it for Amazon or whatever. By doing this, what you're really doing is figuring out what sticks out to the reader. This can be difficult, but learning to divorce yourself enough from your work to get proper perspective on it is an essential skill.

Now, you'll certainly discover that some things are deeply covered, while other things are glossed over. You may also find that in your review, you concentrate on very specific aspects. This a good sign that you may need to go a little broader so that non-experts in the area can make use of the book as well. Look at what you talk about, and then think of someone who has started on that topic only a week before—how would they see it? Would you mention that it was a book for experts? Would you say that it went step-by-step or that it was a good overview? How would you react to your book if you were encountering it for the first time?

Because remember: every reader you get will be encountering it for the first time at some point.

Now, once you've finished your review—and it doesn't need to be more than a paragraph—you need to look at a couple of things. Look at reviews of other books in the topic area you're writing in. How do they compare? Do they mention many of the same things you mention about your book? Do they complain about the books being too general, not giving enough detailed information? Or do they want an easier-to-follow guide? By comparing your review with their reviews of other books, you'll know if you need something of a reshaping.

That can be difficult. You'll then need to look at your outline and see which subsection might need cutting and what larger sections might need expanding. Start by doing that on the outline and do NOT start rewriting yet. Make notes and changes to the outline only, and make detailed notes on why you're making the changes. Do that and you'll have the stage set for the big rewriting that's coming up!

Day 16 – Re-rewriting the Introduction and Chapter 1 – 90 minutes

I know, I've warned you against overworking your piece, but the introduction is so vital that you're going to need several passes at it, especially if you're going to be reworking things rather drastically. You've made your notes, you've decided the new turns you're going to make, and now you're going to make them, but that means you're going to have to at least tweak your intro to reflect these changes. Don't spend too much time on it, you'll likely be using everything you've already written, but try to give it a good spit-shine to make it really glow. Fuss a little about the language at this point, especially since this is the first time you're really trying to put it into a more-or-less final form. Remember that review you wrote? Think of addressing every issue, positive and negative, in your introduction. If you're going to be doing a more detailed and expert-level book, that needs to come across in the introduction, and if you're doing an beginner-level book, that needs to be obvious in the intro. That's why you need to rework it so many times!

After you've done that, work on Chapter 1. This pass, all you want to work on is the language. Find spelling and grammar errors and strengthen up sentences. Look at paragraphs and see if any are huge blocks that can be broken down, or single-sentence ones that can be merged. These will eventually start to pop out at you as you read and reread.

Make the most out of each pass by not overthinking things. You may discover that every time you pass over a particular area of your book, you're always making a change.

That happens to me all the time, and the best way to fight it is to stop doing it! You can choose to focus on particular areas or paragraphs, or even not read the book for meaning, only for spelling. That's never a fun pass, but it's often a necessary one. Sometimes, narrowing your focus, and even purposely skipping over areas, can reap rewards by not bogging you down in the mud.

Remember, the introduction gives you the set-up, but does not function to tell the story of your topic. The first chapter must also set things up, but must do so WHILE telling the tale. That's why you have both, and that's one thing that you must never forget.

Day 17 – Re-researching Chapters 2 and 3 – 90 minutes

This is a tough day, but also one of the more rewarding. You're not really going to be writing today, but what you're going to do is research. You're going to look deep into your piece and see where you need to reference something outside of your text. You can usually tell when you need to do that because you'll see that something is very light, it slips by, leaving little impression. If you can find elements from other sources and sprinkle them in, that's a great way to make your book even more useful.

Start by looking at the resources you referenced in your original search. Go through them to find areas where you think a reference will be useful. Make a note of the publication, date (if you can find it), and the author. There are endless sources for citation formatting, and none's really better than the other. The Chicago Manual of Style is the most widely used but unless you're going to be targeting the academic market, you don't need to go that far.

Three rules of thumb:

1) ALWAYS cite the original work by name and author, at minimum.
2) Unless it's a seminal work, never cite the same publication more than once. This will keep the work from feeling as if it is too beholden to a particular previous publication.
3) Brief is best.

Now, why here and not in your introduction or Chapter 1? Well, those are where you're establishing YOUR voice, and cluttering that up with outside wording can make that a more difficult challenge. You NEED to make it look like this is a work within the topic area you're covering, and doing that without at least referencing work outside your own is very difficult indeed.

You'll want to spend a fair amount of time going over your outline for these chapters. Do these chapters do what you wanted them to do? That's not always easy to see yourself, but if you start looking at outside resources, you'll start to see the areas that tend to get the most coverage, and that's likely where you're going to want to put some emphasis.

Now, I hear you saying, *"But then how do I stand out from the field?"*

The answer is *differences*.

There are a million books about how to lower your golf score. I should know, I've written three of them! They all have the same info: keep your head down, visualize, don't go into sand traps. The reason you can't have just one is that you need the different views. Mine focused on training off-the-course and wise club selection, while the others I found tended to be more centered on the swing instead. The other books tended to be more technical how-to, while mine stayed light and conversational. Finding an element to make your book different is great; just don't go off the rails!

By the way, the third chapter is a great place to insert an extended, relevant personal anecdote.

You're not writing today. You're making notes, preparing references, quotations, and the like. That's all. Today is a lighter day, because tomorrow...well, you'll just have to see about that, won't you?

Day 18 – Foolish Friend Feedback – 120 minutes

Now, let us discover how internally strong you are. Today, you will be tested, tried, and, more than likely, you will find yourself lacking in some dimension. Today is about working through that, and in the end, coming out a better person.

Today, you get back the feedback from the foolish friends you asked to review your book.

It is never easy getting criticism, and if you chose wisely, you'll likely have to deal with criticism. You asked them to be somewhat difficult on your work, right? You asked them to look at your weakest points and comment on how you could improve them, right? You asked them to be critical, and now, you're going to read those criticisms.

Brace yourself.

First off, you'll just read the feedback they send. Ideally, it's in the form of notes on an actual printed copy of the book text. This is the easiest to deal with, as notation in word processing applications, or the "Track Changes" option, is often more complicated than it's worth and can lead to things going unnoticed. Having them take notes, or even write a review like you did a few days ago, can also be very useful.

DO NOT MEET IN PERSON TO DISCUSS THIS!!!!!
I know, you think that if you can talk to them, you can

explain your thinking and they'll get it. You won't have that option when your book is in the wild, so you have to learn to let the work do all the talking for you. If it's not on the page, or screen as it were, it doesn't exist as far as your book is concerned. If you meet, you'll discuss. If you discuss, you'll taint their opinion and it won't be as valid or valuable to you.

Next, read their comments and take notes. If there are a lot of questions, like "What does quasiintellectual mean?" or "What's a cubit?", note that. Often, reviewers will put a largely general overview of the work at the end. It's the way teachers often did in high school. Read that first, if it's there, because that will affect everything. Yes, notes on notes is a bit meta, but you need to put it all down to make sure you've got it. Note anything that comes up more than once, because those are the things that you're blind to seeing in your own work. The entire process should be somewhat painful, but mostly enlightening.

Make sure you review with a couple of different lenses on. The first is for completeness. Did they really get into the nitty-gritty? If they did, you may have to focus on the big picture more yourself in the coming rewrite. If they focused big, you're going to have to be the one who finds the nits to pick and the flyspecks. That's not always a bad thing, because you're more involved with your work, and that's one thing you absolutely need to write books these days: you need to be involved and not just writing on a whim; it needs to be something you DO. Doing beats planning. Planning and doing at the same time, that's where success is really found.

Once you've read the notes your foolish friends have sent to you, drop them a line saying thank you. That's very important. If you're not grateful for them helping you see your work more clearly, then stop writing and go to bed. You're naughty! What they've sent you is the reaction of an audience, and an engaged audience at that. If you can write something that is worth digging deeply in to, then you've done well. If you've created a work that is entirely superficial, then you'll know that too. Getting to know your work is what the third week is largely about. Well, getting to know it and then forcing it to change. THAT'S what the third week is all about.

One more time, you're going to look at your Intro and Chapter 1. Look at what you wrote on the first pass, read it through. Look at your original outline. Absorb everything they have to tell you. Then, read the Foolish Friend notes. After that, read your latest versions of your Intro and Chapter 1. In your reworking, did you address problems that they noticed and you had already caught? That is a very good sign that you understand your readers.

If your foolish friends made notes of a major structural nature, then you have a lot of work to do. Start by looking at the feasibility of what they have said. If your topic is 'How to Write a book in 30 Days' and your foolish friends said, "The days are too structured. Loosen things up," you have to make a decision. You can try to change it altogether, or you can ignore the comment, or you can loosen things up so it FEELS like you've addressed the comment, but really, you've dug your heels in by saying "This is what I'm writing, but I can see that there's a slightly different path up the mountain."

The one thing to never do is blame the reader. They're right, no matter what they say. Even if a comment directly contradicts something that's on the page, they're still right because you must not have been clear enough. When you've written your book, you'll be a non-entity, really. It'll be the work. Approach it like that and you may find yourself with exceptional results.

Day 19 – Rewriting Chapters 2 and 3 – 120 minutes

Again, you're rewriting two chapters, which may seem

daunting, but it's completely doable because, as you are well aware, you haven't stopped thinking about those Foolish Friend comments all night. You stayed up late. You even sat with a ready-to-send email that told your foolish friends off. Only that reminder to be kind to those wonderful readers of yours kept you from sending it. You showed remarkable restraint, and you now know that they were not only right, but doing the best work for you possible—they've helped you see the path you need to take.

Start off by rereading the notes on Chapters 2 and 3. You might want to reread Chapter 1 again as well, but focusing on 2 and 3 is probably a good idea. Start by looking at the comments that were left, and if there was anything more general, like "I was confused by the order of things," start by tackling that one first since it will take the most work to complete.

That specific note is a dangerous one to have to work with. You'll be sorely tempted to simply say that your foolish friends weren't reading closely, but really, they were reading it exactly right. If that's a note you get, start by looking at your outline. How closely did you follow it? That's often where writers get thrown off. They think that the order is so clear that all they have to do is briefly touch on things and it'll all make sense. This is seldom the case.

If your foolish friends went into why they were confused, address that first, but if not, look at the big picture. Where did they get lost? Typically, it has something to do with the way you personally approach whatever the topic is. Like the chef who ALWAYS breaks the eggs and places them in the small glass cup before starting any of the other prep, you have to remember that not everyone does it like that, and you're probably better off going with the more traditional route and mentioning that you do it a bit differently yourself.

When I write a chapter, I always try to give a fluid, logical progression. I do things in ways that people tend to identify with: like days on an imaginary calendar. Looking at your outline, you may find the need to break portions apart and reconfigure, then find the areas where you approached that in the text and move them as well. This may require a bit of transitional rewriting, but it can work. Sometimes, all you need to do is build a scaffolding, add a paragraph that gives a bit more context and clarity to everything around it.

Many writers will say "Cut it 'til it bleeds!" or "Kill your darlings!" about the editing process. I completely disagree when it comes to non-fiction. For the most part, you must provide more than what is in your head to make a topic land fully on your audience, and that means you can't be nearly as lean as some would like. But remember: too wordy is a note a lot of writers get as well. There has to be a balance, and that balance is contained in that foolish friend's reading of your piece. Look for telltale signs of things done right and wrong and you'll come out with a great book.

If a reader says a chapter is "too long," "too dense" or "too convoluted," try working with shorter sentences mixed in. If you express two ideas in a single sentence, turn them into two shorter sentences, and then maybe add another to make it a stand-alone paragraph.

A reader says "hard to follow." At the beginning of each chapter, try adding a brief bit that summarizes what he will find in that chapter. That will act as a guide to the reader and can allow you to be a bit more far-ranging. Plus, it's basically reusing the outline you wrote.

A reader says "What's the point of ____?" That can be a heartbreaker, and will require you to do one of two things—explain or extract. Explaining is simple, just add a bit that explains the purpose of the offending segment for the reader. Extracting is equally simple; you cut out that part. Both can affect the flow of your book and both can be very tricky to do. Sometimes, something as simple as adding a word can make everything clear again.

A reader misses your irony? Yeah, that's never happened to me. I have NOOOOOOOO idea how to make that sort of thing more obvious.

Some will say go through and do the little changes, fixing tense conflicts or spelling and grammar problems. I say tackle the big stuff first, because that will often lead to you cutting and reforming things and the little things fix themselves. Either way can work, though.

Here's the thing about feedback—not every change an early reader mentions needs to be made, but they at least have to be considered. That's the key about external review: you're the writer and the publisher, so in the end, it's up to you, but it's important to take feedback seriously. More often than not, they're right, even when demonstrably wrong.

Do your writing today, and work through the two chapters. Spend some time on your style and maybe even pitch a little humor in to the mix!

Day 20 – Re-research Chapters 4 and 5 – 60 minutes

You know what you're doing now, right? You're confident, certain that you'll complete the fantastic, best-selling book that you've wanted to write ever since you first saw a Kindle. You can do it. No...you WILL do it! A big part of it is understanding that you need to rework things a few times before you hit it right, and you get that now. You've done it more than once. You're going to rock this re-researching of Chapters 4 and 5 with an eye toward tightening up the conclusion.

You did the search for passages to quote and other things you should be noting, but this time, you should look into those resources you've already found and see if there's anything you can incorporate into your book. That's simple.

Basically, do what you did for Chapters 2 and 3 today. That's all.

Day 21 – Rewriting Chapters 4 and 5 – 120 minutes

Yesterday, you got a pep talk. Today, you get writing!

Now, if there were any notes from your foolish friends about the ending, now is the time to do something about it! Work on summation, bringing everything into a tidy little package. You may even want to start by working on Chapter 5 first, and then seeing if there are strings in Chapter 4 that will need restringing.

Let's talk about honing endings, shall we?

The easiest kind of conclusion to write is the Recipe conclusion. "Serves 4 to 6" is all you need to do. For your book, you may need to go a bit deeper. If it's a step-by-step to build a deck, you may want the final chapter to be about something OTHER than actually building the deck. It could be about tips to making your deck last, or ways you can create small improvements over time that will make your deck more usable. You could even look at the deck as a metaphor and write a loving tribute to the deck from the point-of-view of the writer who has now aged and become an old homeowner looking back on all the good times as the rocket-powered cars zoom down the street toward the megalopolis that has grown.

In other words, leave the reader with something to make an impression. It's easy to see that a fun final chapter can turn a reader into a follower. Yes, the Intro was the impression moment, but the go-home chapter is just as important if you're trying to give your readers something memorable.

Again, look at your style in this pass, especially since most of the rest of the work you'll be doing on your book will be of a technical nature. Spend a bit of extra time looking at grammar and spelling, and again, your style. You may discover that you are better at endings than you are at beginnings, or vice versa. Try to work with that.

Today, make sure you have your outline available, because you need to make sure everything is covered. As you read, make sure that every point you had on your outline is covered in your actual text, and if it isn't, figure out if it's because it didn't really fit, which is the least likely, or if you just plain forgot, which is almost always the case.

And just write. You'll be done with the second pass at your amazing book today, the final day of week three. You've done a great job, and you're ready to go toward the final goal with just a bit of work!

Week 4 – Bringing It All Home

You've done it! You've written that book you envisioned! Well played! Week 1, you figured it all out and made a plan. Week 2, you executed and put together the best first draft ever! Week 3, you tore about that crummy first draft and turned it into electronic inky gold! Now, in Week 4, you turn it into a book!

Day 22 – Revenge of the Foolish Friends! – 60 minutes

Today, you're going to be using your foolish friends again, or if possible, a couple of different foolish friends. You have what you think of as your final version of your book and now that you've addressed the first set of Foolish Friend notes, and are still friends with those people, you need to get folks to take a look at your final draft.

Send it out with a couple of notes. First, you want a brisk turnaround. If possible, two days. You want your friends to read it as if they were reading it after they had bought it. You're not looking for them to labor over it, but to look into the book like a book! Then, ask them to write an Amazon-style review of the book for you. Tell them to be honest, even if it means tearing it apart. That sort of honesty can be very useful. Second, tell them to look for something that YOU think is a problem. No author feels that his work is perfect, and there is almost certainly something you want folks to look at. Ask them to look.

Finally, ask what else they would want you to add to the book. This is merely to see if you have a handle on the topic.

Now, spend the time sending out your final draft, be incredibly polite and thankful (even though those friends tore your genius work apart last week), and spend a little time rereading. Don't write today, aside from the request, but read a little and get ready for the more difficult parts of putting it all together.

Day 23 – A Thoroughly Distressing Reread – 120 minutes

Today is all about being incredibly hard on yourself. You're going to do the most thorough reread of your work yet. You are going to read it paragraph by paragraph, noting everything, every word choice, every sentence, EVERYTHING! Then you're going to read it through and make notes on how it felt. Did it flow? Was it well-reasoned? Would you pay to read it? You're going to fuss and fidget and fiddle for two hours today. You will have arguments with yourself over whether or not a specific word was correct, whether you made your point clearly enough. You are going to assume that you are wrong at every turn and then have to try to convince yourself that you were right. You will be playing devil's advocate to yourself.

You have concerns about what you've done, no doubt, and here, briefly, you are going to give into them and work like you have no idea if you've done the right thing. As you work in this mode, you'll either find faults, and then quickly fix them, or realize that you've been doing OK all along. That's the purpose of this day. You will want to tear your book apart. You will start working on it again in your head, and you will have every fear that this is actually the worst piece of writing ever committed. And as you are re-re-rereading, you'll start to see things that jump out at you as strong, intelligent, wise, even brilliant. These things will start to string together. You'll see the effort paying off, and it will bolster you and make it all come into focus: this is a good piece, the best piece you could possibly do!

Then, you need to throw everything away! No more looking at the outline. From here on out, the text isn't 100% final, but what you have is more or less what'll be in the final book.

Have you thought of a brilliant title for your book yet? I never start with titles, but they tend to reveal themselves somewhere around the final edit and you'll probably find it lurking in your text as well. You certainly want to avoid something as simple as "Menu Planning" or "Drywalling Your Carport," while also not going too out there with titles like "A Meal Made of Promise" or "To Hang the Eternal Walling." Try to come up with something that works for your intended audience.

Day 24 – The Search for Art – 90+ minutes

This is the road toward a book that will attract attention. One thing that books make easy is using art to help illustrate points. If you're doing a step-by-step book, taking a photo of your project along the way will help make everything clearer. If you're doing a more general book, a photo can give context that will help draw readers in further. A good photo, or even a decent drawing, really makes your book pop!

The first thing you should do is to search for photos. Google makes it easy right now (and likely in the future) by allowing you to search for photos and then search within those results by size. You're probably going to want 'Large' photos, though 'Medium' photos can work as well. Then, there's an option to search within different Usage types. The one you want to select is "Labeled for Reuse," which means you can use the images wherever you want, however you want. OK, I know it's not quite as easy as all that, but for the most part, those are images you can use for free, and you should mine those for illustrations.

While that's the easiest way, there are other forms of illustrations you can try. The first, and especially good if you are doing a step-by-step book, is to take your own photos. These are certainly free to use and they'll allow you the most control over the photos' focus. The downside is that they're often not of professional quality. There are also illustration books and clip art, both available online and in actual book form. These can work, but finding exactly what you're looking for is harder.

The key to art for your book is that it has to be professional-looking, accurately illustrative, and, ideally, it has to add something to the text. Sometimes, imagery just to break up the monotony of paragraph after paragraph of heavy wordage is a good idea, but it has to give something back in the way of content.

The reason it's 90 minutes plus today is simple: you're going to want to keep at it. Once you start looking into these things, the tendency is to go and go and go. And today, I'm encouraging that! This is the time to explore and have a little fun before the hard work starts again!

Day 25 – The Foolish Friends Strike Back! – 120 minutes

You've got all the feedback you're ever going to get before this thing hits the presses. You have to get it all together to make it into the final final FINAL product. First, you should start by doing exactly what you did with your first Foolish

Friend review, but more importantly, you should try to see only the major problems as things to deal with. Your friends will likely catch a few more typos and point out some grammatical problems. Heck, they might even say, "This is GREAT! I want more!" It doesn't really matter what they say; you need to hear it and you need to take it seriously. That doesn't mean you have to address every problem they point out, but you do need to take them all seriously and address the bigger problems. If you get a note like "You need a better ending or the reader's going to get lost," then you really need to think about that one, and if there's something really small, like a misplaced comma, that's an easy fix. But other stuff can likely slide. You want this feedback to help you understand what readers want, like, and see.

Now, after this, your document is completely locked. Eyes have seen it, you've been over it with a fine-toothed comb, and you have investigated every aspect outside your book. You're done with the writing, but not with the book. The next step is a lot of fun, but can be a bit painful for the first-timer.

Day 26 – Laying It All Out – 120 minutes

At this point, you have the text done and you have some images to go along with it. Now you have to put it into a form where you can turn it into a book. The first thing you should do is decide what form of book you're going to do. For example, if you want your book to be available on Kindle, you'll need to use something like Kindle Direct Publishing, which will pretty much only give you something that can be used on the Kindle. You might find a program like inDesign by Adobe or iBook Publisher more convenient for creating multiple platform books, though none of these will be all things to all would-be publishers.

There are some good formats to consider. ePub is pretty much universal on eReaders, and most (though not all) layout programs will let you output to ePub. Some, like iBook Author, will even let you take an ePub created in another program and convert it into an iBook, which can be made available on the iTunes bookstore. PDF also has its place, especially on sites like Scribd and Issuu, and it can be read on almost any device or in Web browsers. Smashwords, meanwhile, allows you to create works out of Microsoft Word documents in various formats for various devices. It's as close to a one-stop-shop as you're going to find when it comes to books.

In all honesty, just pick one and go with it. That's really the best way. Some folks will work better in one program or another. I tend to like inDesign or iBooks Author even though I understand that one is an atomic flyswatter, far too powerful a tool for what I need to do, and the other is pretty much just for a niche I want to fill. Find one and spend a little time just reading up on it and learning the requirements. Some will only let you do text, while others are far more flexible. Consider that when you're looking into what to go with.

As soon as you have become familiar with your chosen program, get to work! You're likely not going to finish today, but work for a while and get the hang of things.

Day 27 – Work it! – 120 minutes

Yesterday you spent a lot of time getting to know your program, and today you're going to start really working on putting your book together. You'll find a few hiccups here and there, and you'll probably make a hash of everything at least once, but it's OK. You've saved your text in multiple places, so it'll be safe no matter how much you muck with it!

Some tips for layout:

If you're working with a program that allows photos, try to

place the images in a way that will not require the readers to bounce around the photos to keep up with the flow of the text. Nothing infuriates me more than having an image plopped in the middle of a paragraph, requiring me to bounce all around it.

If you're working in a text-only form, lay it out once then output it. See if it matches what you want when it comes to indentation, spacing, text formatting, etc. This can be extremely frustrating and often will add half-again the time to laying out and finishing a book.

Do not be afraid to use templates! Most programs have templates you can choose from for the format of your book. These can make things much easier, but are a bit stiffer. These are great for first-timers who are new to layout.

So, get to it! Work, work, work!

Day 28 – Fussing over it – 120 minutes

OK, you're just going to keep doing your preparations, and by now, you're probably either done or nearly there. The important thing is not to needle your work so much that you ruin it. It is difficult to know when to give it up and let it alone, but here are some hints.

If you find yourself finishing, then exporting your book and reading it, then adding another element, and then exporting again, leading to reading again, and then adding another element on and on ad infinitum, you've got a problem and it's likely that you're not actually adding anything important to the book.

If you insist that every paragraph has a photo to go with it, that's a difficult matter. You should only do that if you're doing a step-by-step and need to give visual confirmation of every move. An image a page, or a couple per chapter, is probably enough.

If you're going back through your book and find that you're making changes to each and every sentence, you're probably overdoing it. If you notice a spelling mistake in each and every sentence, you probably skipped Week 3.

If you're more concerned with how your book looks than what it says, you're probably looking at it wrong. Remember: people READ books for the text first; layout and imagery are secondary, though can help put things in better perspective.

And now you're done with the creation process. You've created it—a book!—though you're not quite done yet. You have two more days!

Week 5 – The One-Day Week

Day 29 – What You Hath Wrought!

You're done with it. You're ready to go and get it out to where people can see it! You have a lot of places you can get it out—some for free, others where you can set a price. No matter what you do, you should take a few steps to make sure people see your book.

First, as always, is social media. If you have a Twitter, Facebook, Instagram, Tumblr or any other sort of social media presence, make sure that folks know you've written a book. Don't talk about it much while you're writing it. Many writers find that talking about the book ends up taking precedence over actually writing it, and that can derail you. When you release it, put up links to where folks can find it. Don't bash people over the head with it, but try to make sure folks know it's there. I suggest one post a day for the first week, then a post every other day for the next two weeks, and then a post when there's something else that relates to it in the news. That way, you will not feel like a self-aggrandizing jerk.

Another is no matter what system you use to get your book out there, you must give as much information as possible on the site. Metadata, as it's called, will help your book be found by people searching for it. Author name, title, subject, and so on. Make sure you fill out the fields as completely as you can. Give readers as many ways as possible to find your book.

If you have a Web site, make sure to put links to your book on it. If you have friends who are big readers, get them to talk about your book in places like Goodreads or Reddit. Don't be afraid to ask folks to help you get the word out. Some of the biggest-selling books of all time were based on word of mouth.

And remember: no matter what, it isn't going to become a best-seller immediately. Some books wait for years to sell a dozen copies, and then something happens that causes sales to boom! Sometimes, a book will not sell a single copy. These books aren't failures (and I'll admit that I sometimes go out of my way to find and read them!), but they just didn't have drive behind them to turn them into top sellers. You can do everything right, and it just might not find an audience. These things happen, but there is an audience for everything, and if you get the word out, you'll likely find it, and once you have found one audience, you can tap into more!

Day 30 – Sit Back and Relax!

Now, the most important thing: celebrate your victory! There is a tradition I have where I drink a single beverage after I hit 'Publish'. If I'm ghostwriting a book on golf, I am likely to pop open a lovely cider since it reminds me of a walk on the course. If I'm writing a guidebook to New York City, I will certainly pop open a seltzer! Think about this while you're writing and come up with something that you'll reward yourself with when you finish your book. Having a goal to work toward, no matter how silly it may seem, can be a great incentive. I know a writer whose writing always ends with a trip to a comic book shop where he buys the latest

Archie comic. He's weird, but it works for him.

It's been a pleasure writing for you! I hope when you finish your best-selling book, you'll remember to mention me in the acknowledgments!

About the Author

Amy Pendergrass is a bestselling author who helps people get unstuck and be unstoppable in every area of their lives. Getting more from life and your business doesn't need to be complicated.

Amy believes simplicity is the key to your personal power, productivity, inner peace, and crystal-clear clarity.

In her books, Amy gives actionable plans for simplifying your life, staying organized and productive so you can get what you truly want out of life.

So instead of reading overhyped strategies that rarely work in the real world, you'll get information that can be easily and immediately implemented.

When not writing, Amy likes to read, exercise, make healthy meals for her family, and explore the different parts of the world.

Check out Amy Pendergrass' other book *Declutter Your life in 29 Days: A Minimalist Approach To Clear Your Home, Mind and Schedule.*

Made in United States
Orlando, FL
13 May 2024

46795008R00036